Church Unusual
For the Exceptional Leader

Oscar & Crystal Jones

Copyright © 2016 Oscar & Crystal Jones

All rights reserved.

ISBN: 1936867168
ISBN 13: 978-1-936867-16-5

Dedications

To Agape Pastors & Leaders

Jake & Keila Allen

Greg & Saryta Colbert

Eric & Wanda Daniel

Cleaver Davis

John & Minnie Hardy

Thomas & Brenda Hooks

David & Pamela Houston

James & Michelle Stapleton-Morris

Kenneth & Adrienne Nears

Esosa & Shereena Osai

Portia McGee Parchman

Aseneth Peek Parker

Tony & Aries Winans

CONTENTS

	Acknowledgments	i
One	You're Not Normal	1
Two	No More Church as Usual	7
Three	Sizing Up The Ministry	19
Four	The Unconventional Marriage	27
Five	The Heart of Ministry	37
Six	Accountability	47
Seven	Managing Church Finances	51
Eight	Burning or Burnout?	61
Nine	Engaging Membership	69
Appendix	The Pastor's Library	77

ACKNOWLEDGMENTS

We give all glory and honor to the most Exceptional Leader of all time, Jesus Christ.

~One~
You're Not Normal

If you are new to the ministry, congratulations on accepting the call. It is an honor and a great privilege to work for the Lord. You have embarked on an exciting adventure. There will be ups and downs, challenges and opportunities; nevertheless the reward in ministry is like none other. You have decided to agree with God by serving His people. That decision will not go unrewarded.

Maybe you have been at it for a while. If that is the case, you may be coming to this book for encouragement, insight, or strength. While ministry leadership is a tough career, you must always remember that the sacrifice is NEVER greater than the reward. God will always give more to you than you give to Him. So purpose to give Him your best and give Him your all.

No matter where you are in your service to God, new to ministry or a veteran - thank you for saying yes. There are never too many pastors, bishops, apostles, etc. We need laborers for the harvest. It's ripe for the picking.

Church unusual is about changing our approach to kingdom work, outside of the established norms. It's for those leaders who tend to color outside of the lines of what is acceptable. And the only type of leader who can do that is one that is discontent with mediocre. He is not your average Joe. Nor is he a hireling. There is too much at stake. He understands the responsibility of his assignment. He is called not to just preach the word. He is called to make disciples. He feels he must reach the lost before it's too late.

The call of ministry leader is for the brave. It's for those that are full of courage. It's a unique call. The mission is to help people believe the unbelievable and to help them see what is not already clear. It is his aim to teach people to be more than what they are: This exceptional leader is passionate about his call and sees it as more than a duty; it's what he or she was born to do. There is nothing more rewarding in the world for him/her. It is an extraordinary charge. Shouldn't that be expected? An extraordinary call from an extraordinary God. He desires that we would not settle in for the status quo. He wants us to move beyond average. He doesn't want us to flow in mediocrity. In Him, we are created with the capacity for amazing.

Now to him who is able to do exceeding abundantly above all that we ask or imagine, according to his power that is at work within us, Ephesians 3:20

Most people live below their capacity, limited by fears, ignorance, false information, etc. Leaders are commissioned to help them move beyond their limitations.

Pastors are captains so to speak, front-runners of God's people. We are not called to be common warriors. The scriptures say MORE than a conqueror. We are to compel

His people to victory in the personal and corporate wars that they must fight. We have voluntarily enlisted for this army. We have signed up for active duty. We are on the frontlines with God's people behind us. We rush forward to battle, running through a troop and leaping over a wall. (Psalm 29:18)

The assignment is not easy. It takes someone pretty special to be an effective ministry leader. It is by far the toughest job on earth. Clergy enter people's lives in a way that no other profession does. We are there when they are at their lowest (sickness, loss of loved ones, unemployment, etc.) ...And at their highest (weddings, graduations, new births). We have the awesome privilege to walk beside them as their cheerleader and coach. We get to observe them grow and mature and witness transformation up close and personal. Indeed this call is not a common one.

God's chosen leader is an original. He/she doesn't try to copy another clergy leader or preach someone else's sermons.

God is so unique he creates each person with a different fingerprint. Even identical twins do not have the same thumb print. Over the years, snow has fallen and it has been said that each individual snowflake has its own design. In the same way, we all are completely different. So the extraordinary leader draws on God's spirit for His/her own pattern. He uses his/her own individuality and creativity to build an unusual church.

Unusual churches are Bible-based and not tradition based. They are not quiet and compliant. They are formed to turn the world upside down; to shake some things up. They are much more effective than their conventional counterparts. They tend to draw people with the love of Christ. They don't put new wine into old wineskins. Unusual churches with extraordinary leaders tend to make people feel uncomfortable in their religion. It's not done on purpose. But it is just a part of who they are. They embrace the lost instead of shunning them. Homosexuals and fornicators are welcomed guests in their churches. They aren't required to get their lives right first. Neither do they have to fit into religious cliques. **However the unusual church invites and welcomes the outcast without sacrificing truth.** The truth is still exalted. The unusual church feels no pressure to compromise.

Often the unusual congregation is what the conventional would call – misfits. There is not one personality type that makes up their churches, but a collage of people. The wealthy and the poor, the educated and the uneducated, the faithful and the unfaithful all gather together to worship God. They come from all walks of life: bikers, business men, ex-cons, strippers, nurses, etc. Tattoos, colored hair and piercings don't offend those called to build God's kingdom. All are welcome. It has to be the Word that changes the people, not the rules. We are free to reach out to drug dealers and gang bangers – offering them something different. Our collective call is to do what Jesus did – He embraces the ones that ordinary churches reject.

In St. Matthew 11:19 The Son of Man came eating and drinking, and they say, 'Here is a glutton and a drunkard, a friend of tax collectors and sinners.' <u>But wisdom is proved right by her deeds</u>.

The bridegroom is coming back for His bride, and there is nothing customary about her. We must break away from the routine and traditional to be exceptional. That's what

God desires. He is an excellent God therefore he will produce an excellent church composed of excellent people.

So, leader, know that God has created you for this time in history, right here, right now. You were born to make a difference. He equipped you with gifts, talents and abilities to advance his kingdom. You were created to make an impact wherever God has positioned you. He chose you to lead his people. What an honor! So do it well. Make Him smile. Don't worry what others will say. God is the one who has called you. Follow Him.

~Two~

No More Church as Usual

You've heard this phrase probably a million times. 'No more church as usual'. It's become quite the cliché. We are implying that something is going to be different or abnormal. But usually the change in the church is so insignificant that you can barely see a difference, if any at all. When something is 'unusual' it's so markedly different that it causes one to stop and take notice. Unusual is defined as bizarre, unfamiliar, odd, unconventional, and curious. Can you imagine if your church were described in that way? Is it a compliment? We think so. The church has fallen into some pretty repetitious patterns. And we bore the people with our routine. So the unusual church is awake. It's radical. Her behavior makes you want to go check the Bible to see if it lines up. She will cause you to think again.

The unconventional church will break traditions and upset the status quo. Radical in nature, she is brave enough to stand out. She rebels against religion and refuses to do what is expected of her. In fact, it often seems she does just the opposite. She shakes up the culture with her extreme posture. And she becomes a magnet to the world.

Jesus' ministry was pretty radical in His time. He purposely chose to heal on the Sabbath Day which was strictly forbidden. Traditions were less important than man. That was the message he wanted to get across. Hanging out with the ostracized, caused the religious rulers to look down on Him. Nevertheless He did what was necessary. He seemed to oppose every Pharisaical taboo. He stood against every tradition of man without ever breaking God's law. He was the most peculiar leader of all time. And yet, there is no ministry more effective than His.

It is not productive to be unconventional simply for the sake of being unconventional. But your ministry should be radical for the sake of Christ. The unusual ministry lays its foundation in following Jesus. Everything else flows from that basis. The uncommon leader is so outlandish that he preaches what Jesus says (politically correct or not). There is no fear in his blood. He trusts God completely and boldly operates completely within the context of His word. He never loses sight of his mission.

The Bible is God's dangerous book. Think about it. There are some pretty extreme principles written in those pages. In fact, it's so outrageous that most people struggle to believe it. Most have not even attempted to read it completely. It's too edgy, too intense. It's over the top.

Can you imagine if Christians would actually follow the Bible? If they were to 'love and do good to their enemies', what would happen? That's some revolutionary doctrine. It's enough to shake you out of your slumber. It's such a strange precept that many question whether it's even possible. However we know God never asks us to do anything that he does not empower us to do.

If we yearn to experience the power of God and see miracles, signs and wonders. We must do the outlandish. We must sow something different in order to reap something different. We cannot continue doing the same old thing day in and day out while expecting something novel. We can't continue our ineffective habits. We must not revel over yesterday's trophies. It's a brand new day.

Consider the story of Samson. In Judges 15:14 When he came to Lehi, the Philistines came shouting to meet him. *Then the Spirit of the LORD rushed upon him*, and the ropes that were on his arms became as flax that had caught fire, and his bonds melted off his hands. ¹⁵ And he found a fresh jawbone of a donkey, and put out his hand and took it, and with it he struck 1,000 men.

When Samson defeated the Philistines with the jawbone of a donkey, the scriptures tells us in Judges 15:17 As soon as he had finished speaking, he threw away the jawbone out of his hand. And that place was called Ramath-lehi. He didn't think to himself, "This is how I must secure victory every time". He knew the power wasn't in the jawbone. It was the Spirit of the Lord. He didn't create an idol or tradition out of the jawbone. In that same way, we should not get locked in old methods, but we must lean on the Spirit of God. The power is not in the method or the jawbone, it's in obedience to God. Following the leading of God will cause us to be victorious every time.

Sometimes very traditional churches think that they are unusual or proclaim, "No More Religion." Unfortunately we all generally conduct church in the same manner. We hold Bible study on Tuesday or Wednesday evening and Sunday school on Sunday morning using the same Sunday School books. Our order of service is basically the same. We have the same annual events. We sing the same songs and preach the same sermons. So what's so unusual about church? Typically, nothing. The worst part of it is, when one of our colleagues venture into the realm of the unusual, we squawk and say ,"It's not God". It makes us feel uncomfortable when things aren't the same. We become like the Pharisees. We defy change, even if it's for our good.

God is so amazing. He is multidimensional and multi-faceted. He is unique and creative. He does not wish to produce carbon copy churches. Just as he makes every person on the earth different. We must allow God to give us the pattern for our particular congregation. God desires that each ministry have its own flavor.

There are more than 5 billion people on the earth who do not know Christ. There is not one church on earth that will be attractive to all. God has sent different personalities with different ministry gifts and styles to lead different churches to reach all people. We can be far more effective if we use God's pattern and not someone else's to win the lost. We should not get trapped with doing what we are used to seeing. God is calling us to do something innovative. Something distinctive. It's time for a shift.

We say no more church as usual but we have to get to the place where we mean it. We must be brave enough and bold enough to do what God says and not what man expects.

As we follow the Holy Spirit, the kingdom of God will shift in such a magnificent way. We will see the signs and miracles. We will see whole families saved and entire cities healed. It's time to get out of the box and back into the Book.

Certainly at our foundation is His Word of Truth. However the methods and techniques should be diverse. We get so caught up in the cookie cutter pattern that we do not even question whether the assigned Sunday School book has the lessons that God wants taught this quarter to this particular group of people.

We purchase Vacation Bible School or Children's Church curriculum because someone recommended it to us. Is our church really unusual? Are we following the leading of the Spirit? If so, that's great! But if not, it's tragic.

We should never just follow a pattern, of doing what others did before us. God is certainly not asking us all to teach the same lesson, the same week, and in exactly the way it is laid out in our purchased materials. We all have different spiritual needs, challenges, and learning styles. There are different spirits that challenge a particular region. We must be in tuned to the Spirit of God to know what is necessary. The Berean and the Corinthian church did not have the same needs. Paul wrote different letters to them with different messages.

If we can break out of the religious box, we could see better results. Church would not be boring. More people would "want" to come and want to participate. We would see spiritual growth in a way that we haven't seen it.

The first step to change is to examine our motives. We must question why we do some of the things that we do. Is it in line with scripture? Does the Bible demand it or is it "church tradition"? Has God told me to do this or is it what I know to do?

Let's shake what we've seen in the past and challenge

ourselves. Let's allow God to renew our minds to align our thoughts with his.

Just Imagine....

What if we didn't confine communion to the first Sunday of every month? Or we were free enough to not wear white? We could have communion as we feel led by the Lord. It could be held midweek or every week. We could take communion in our homes and on our jobs.

What if instead of Sunday School, we had Saturday School or Thursday School? Maybe you would have more people available to teach and more willing to attend.

What if we created our own lessons for Sunday School instead of using the standard books? (Or what if we had someone to create the lessons for us who could write down exactly what we felt like God was saying). Perhaps we would see the people grow at a faster pace.

What if we alternated instructors, instead of letting the same person teach year after year? We could give everyone an opportunity to teach, including teenagers. (We do learn better by teaching).

What if we let the children lead prayer in church and help collect the offering? They would feel included and feel affirmed. Maybe it would draw them in.

What if baptism was hosted at a local hotel or park? And what if the candidates didn't have to wear white? Maybe more people would attend your baptism service.

What if we served dinner before Bible Study and breakfast before Sunday morning worship? That would make it more convenient for families to get to service.

Once you start reasoning like that, you will unlock your unconventional thinking. You become undone and your religion begins to unravel. There will be a shifting in your spirit. Yes, it's time to rethink church.

Here are some unusual activities of our church.

We have hosted a picnic for the homeless. We took our grills to the section of town where they commune and barbecued hamburgers and hotdogs just for them. They seem to come from everywhere. And they were always so appreciative.

Who says shopping cannot be a time of ministry? Our church hosted a shop and share event. The ladies went shopping to buy a gift in her own size for a woman confined to a shelter. The gifts were beautifully wrapped and presented at a luncheon held especially in their honor.

We have gone out on the streets of Detroit to give roses to prostitutes. We gave them cards that said God loves you and has a plan for your life. We also gave them information to get out of the life they were in. Some cried. Some held the flowers to their hearts. They welcomed our prayer. It not only impacted them but it impacted us. We were humbled.

We've ministered to seniors in nursing homes and group homes. We had our children's ministry go and sing songs and make Valentines for them.

We also have given out hats, gloves and scarves to those homeless standing on street corners.

We held Family Life Academy instead of traditional Bible study. We offered about 4 to 5 courses per 6 week semester. Members could sign up for which class they needed.

We've hosted a Kids Conference for kids only. No adults allowed (except staff). The children had workshops presented through skits, puppet shows and a clown. Toys (donated by a major department store) were given away every 5 minutes.

We do not only have pastor appreciation service, we have congregation appreciation service. We give gifts to every member at anniversary. We also have an appreciation dinner for everyone who serves in the ministry.

We have asked who in the congregation has nothing to give. We have them come up and allow the congregation to sow financially into them. We have also had times where everyone just randomly gave an offering to someone else in the service.

We hosted a Reunion Service to invite back former members. Each former member was given a gift for the time they were a part of the ministry. We thanked them for whatever time and talent they invested in our ministry. Some renewed their membership.

We suspend Bible study in the summer months and hit the streets.

How about drive-thru prayer? A pastor friend of ours hosts a time of drive-thru prayer. People drove up to the church in their cars between certain hours for prayer. They didn't have to get out of their cars. They had people positioned in the drive-way to pray for them.

Another church leader does not have a regular Bible study. His Bible study is conducted at a senior citizen's facility. The members show up to serve the elderly.

Another church carries bag lunches in their cars to hand out to the homeless who ask for food.

Another church has their Worship Service not just on Sunday but they offer a Saturday option.

What will your church do? Is God asking you to do something different? When church is unusual, we can do amazing things.

What if we were willing to share…

And partner with other churches….not necessarily of the same denomination? Geez, that's unheard of, you say? Thank you. That's what God is calling for – ground breaking ministry. He wants us to do something out of the ordinary.

We've hosted a women's conference as a 5 church collaboration. All 5 churches shared in the duties and the ministry. It was amazing. The power of God rested in that place like something we had not experienced. God smiled.

We invite other churches to share in our baptism. We host it at the local YMCA. We pay the fee. And they just bring their people and join with us. No cost to them. Each pastor baptizes as he chooses. And God shows up. Isn't that the spirit of God?

What if we were willing to share our resources with other Christian churches? Let smaller churches share your building. Allow the church down the street to use your parking lot. Let churches that need chairs and tables borrow yours. If the church we shepherd is God's church and the resources are His, then why not?

Let's stretch a little further. Let's get a little more fanatical.

What if we shared people?

Are we making you uncomfortable yet? We want you to be pulled out of your coziness. They are not your people anyway. They belong to God. So If a smaller church was hosting an event and needed ushers/hostesses, or a cleaning crew why not ask your team to serve? What if pastors weren't possessive over God's people? If you have a praise team or dance ministry, why not let them serve at another ministry? Not just when you are the invited speaker, but when there is a real need.

What if several churches banded together to go out into our neighborhoods to share the love of Christ? Offering to help rake leaves, or clean or do some other chore? What if we weren't in competition with one another? And a group of pastors got together and went to each other's churches to pray?

What if we were truly the body of Christ advancing not just a church but a kingdom? How would that look? I think we would strike a match and start a real revolution. Too often, leaders have had to work hard to get what they have because no one was willing to share. And unfortunately we continue the selfish cycle. Let's break through and break forth. Freely we have received, let us give to each other freely.

We have over 5 billion people to reach, let's utilize every resource available. Let's not knock what some other Christian church is doing. We are all on the same team. We must be about our Father's business.

So many people, so little time.

OSCAR & CRYSTAL JONES

~Three~
Sizing Up the Ministry

When we first start out in ministry, most of us dream of leading a mega ministry. We want to see people come to God by the thousands. There is nothing wrong with that idea...if our motives are right. However EVERY PASTOR WILL NOT LEAD A MEGA MINISTRY. The exceptional leader understands this and accepts it.

According to an article in Leadership Journal, of all the churches in the world, ninety percent are below 200 people in membership. That's a significant statistic. The small church makes up 90% of all churches. So there is NO WAY, we can all lead a mega ministry. The article asks us to consider if the small church is God's *strategy* rather than a problem.

Every person doesn't fit into a mega ministry. Some people are better suited to smaller ministries with a family type atmosphere. Many baby boomers (born post WWII - 1963) have a hard time with a mega ministry. They don't like the big screens and sometimes impersonal feel. They are loyal people. They don't change churches as easily as their children (the Millennials)

Others love to be in a crowd and will thrive in a mega

setting. Those are the Millennials aka Generation X's (born between early 60's and early 80's) and Generation Y's (born 1980-2000) who are more apt to plug into a mega church. They are techy and like all the uses of technology that the mega church utilizes.

Our charge is to reach out to souls. This is the life of the church. Certainly we should always be looking to win more. However, a ministry leader is wise enough to <u>not</u> consider himself a failure if he does not reach a certain number. He knows and understands that the numbers are all up to God. He is willing to lead whatever size church God assigns him.

Ministry is **never** about how many people we serve. If that was the case, we could really get puffed up as the number increases. The scripture clearly humbles us with this reminder, 1 Corinthian 3:6-8   I planted the seed, Apollos watered it, but God has been making it grow. ⁷ So neither the one who plants nor the one who waters is anything, but only God, who makes things.

God alone decides how many we will serve. He knows how much we can handle. And it's not so that we can brag to our ministry colleagues or even feel good about ourselves. Ministry success is strictly defined by our willingness to obey God.

Effectiveness should be measured in spiritual growth, not in physical bodies or numbers on a roll.

We have seen many ineffective mega pastors and many amazing successful pastors with smaller ministries. So the size of the ministry does not determine its success. King David got in trouble with God for numbering the people.

I Chronicles 21:11 Satan rose up against Israel and incited

David to take a census of Israel.

Numbers can cause men to feel good about themselves. They begin to rely on their own strength instead of leaning on the Lord. When the numbers are increased there is the potential to actually become glory stealers, thinking higher of ourselves than we ought. We cannot use the number of followers as the measure of success. Cult Leader Jim Jones had over 900 followers. Certainly we do not deem him successful.

In the same way, when the numbers decrease, some leaders feel bad, as if they have failed because people leave the ministry or they just have not seen the growth that they would like to see. God has called pastors to serve churches of different sizes. Each ministry is unique. Be who God calls you to be. Don't strive to be more or less than we ought. God has a vision. We simply need to follow it.

Our eyes should be set on building a strong, healthy church, not a big one.

We are not talking brick and mortar or even the concept of church. The church is the body of believers. It's people that matter, not the institution.

Take note of an unconventional pastor who had a very small congregation. His name is Noah. Noah had a congregation of 7 and they were all his family. No one else was interested in joining his ministry. His message was too negative and extreme. He was preaching about rain, something the earth had never experienced.

Noah chose holiness at a time when the rest of the world chose sin. God found a faithful man in Noah. Because he walked with God, he could be trusted. It takes a man convinced of who God is to do what Noah did. While the whole earth was going crazy in their sin, drenching themselves in immorality, he chose righteousness.

Noah preached for 120 years that it was going to rain. And NO ONE believed his message other than his family. Yet Noah was highly successful.

Noah had an unusual task to fulfill. God asked him to do something no one else had ever done. He had to design and build an ark; something he had never seen for something that he had never experienced - rain. Can you imagine building a boat, when you don't even know what a boat looks like? This ark was 450 feet long, 75 feet wide and 45 feet high, with 3 stories. And he built it by hand. There were no fancy machines, or factories. Everything, every room had to be carved out by hand. This giant contraption would need to be able to float once water hit the ground. Here this mere man was used by God in an enormous way. God trusted him with this massive task knowing that Noah would obey. There would be many opportunities to give up. But Noah would hold fast to the word.

Noah had to go against the culture. There was so much corruption and wickedness on the earth. There probably were other preachers. However no one else was preaching about water falling from the sky. It had never happened before. And all the while Noah was preaching, he was nailing together these planks. The people must've counted him as a local nut. They probably laughed at him. They mocked him. They jeered him. And he still had to go year after year preaching the same "ridiculous" message. God could trust him to keep going. He knew that Noah would not quit.

Noah had to possess ridiculous faith. Part of Noah's assignment was to gather a large number of animals onto this ark. The earth was so wicked that God wanted to destroy the animals as well (Gen 6:7). However he had to preserve some of every species. Now how do you get a lion to get into the ark without turning the cows into hamburger? But somehow these animals did not attack one another. There was a different spirit on that ark. Noah never thought to question God whether this was sensible. The scriptures just said, he did according to **ALL** that God commanded him. (Gen 6:22)/ Now, that's pretty radical.

Noah was faithful to his God despite what it looked like. Noah was 500 when he begat Shem, Ham and Jepheth (5:32) (6:10). Noah preached for over 120 years that it was going to rain (7:6). Year after year, nothing happened. He didn't know when God's promise would come to pass. But he knew that God always keeps his word. He saw no progress. People got worse. And nobody joined his "Church of the Ark". The ministry was not growing. After 5 years, After 15, 40, 50, 70 and even in the 100th year, he only had 7 converts (his wife, his 3 sons and their wives).   Many pastors today would say Noah was ineffective. But God said he was faithful. Faithfulness denotes success, not numbers.

Noah was successful because of his obedience to God. Now just suppose Noah got discouraged because he only had 7 to follow him? What if he shut down the ministry? What if he had given up on building the ark? And all because someone asked him the unimportant question of "How many people are in your church?" He would have failed. Success and failure in ministry are measured simply by our willingness to obey God.

Moses led a mega church. But it would not be

productive to compare Moses and Noah's ministries. Their assignments were different. If you are going to be an exceptional leader, you must follow His specific assignment for your life. You would be remiss to measure yourself by someone else's ministry.

Effectiveness will cause you to lose your popularity. Preach and live God's message and some will leave. They will be offended because of the Word and the numbers will fluctuate. Understand that people come and go. Jesus even endured a church split because of his teachings.

From this time many of his disciples turned back and no longer followed him. John 6:66

The 70 walked with him no more. Jesus turned to the 12 and asked "Will you leave also?" He went from 82 to 12. He lost nearly 85% of his following. Was Jesus' ministry effective? Of course, it was and still is today. His ministry has transcended generations.

God is after the remnant, not the crowd.

Remember: Jesus said how they treated me is how they will treat you. So let's remember what is important and what is not. Make sure you are giving those that you serve the true word of God and that you are following the same. Then He will say, "Well done, my good and faithful servant. Enter into the joy of the Lord!"

Is there ever a time that we should count the people? Sure. Some churches count the number of people who give their lives to Christ. Some count the number of people who get baptized or the number that join themselves to the ministry. Numbers are tracked for different purposes. Often if a church is trying to get a bank loan, the bank will require that they know how many people are committed to the ministry. They will have to be able to separate those numbers from children and adults. Pastors track numbers to see if a process is effective.

Acts 2:41…stated that 3000 were added to the church. So somebody counted people. However, it wasn't for one man's boasting, rather it was to show what God was doing. His church had been activated. And here was the first harvest.

The main thing is not to get caught up in the numbers – feeling good about yourself when they rise and bad about yourself when they drop. It is the spirit of pride that allows us to attach the numbers to our self-worth. The unusual pastor does not vacillate when the numbers are up or down. He understands and accepts that God alone is in charge. The Lord works through his designated leaders to bring His desired result. It's God's work and He is the one responsible for the numbers. As leaders, we are to simply do what He asks. That's what makes us successful.

~Four~
The Unconventional Marriage

Have you ever seen clergy lovers - a pastor and his wife passionately in love? It is sad to say that it is rare. Nevertheless you can find them walking hand in hand. He is wildly in love with his bride and she with him. They can hardly keep their hands off one another. He publicly declares his love for her and she does the same. His romantic gaze and her comfortable smile lets everyone know that all is well in their home. The two are more than lovers, they are friends. Each respects the other.

They are not perfect but their love is. They allow room for mistakes. Both apologize regularly just to keep their love from souring. They keep interfering intruders out of their private love affair. He doesn't allow anyone to harm her or speak ill of her. She won't hear the slightest complaint about him. Her love covers his faults. She offers her strength to the areas that he is weak. He accepts her help as an extension of himself. They diligently work to protect their love.

The two continuously take time to squander on their love. They date regularly and get away often. It seems as if they are always on some type of extended honeymoon.

The fragrance of their love is so strong that it is contagious and finds itself spilling over to the other marriages in the congregation. Yes, the message to all who attend their ministry is that marriage is good, fun and exciting. And isn't that the way God designed it?

Certainly marriage is not easy. But nothing worth having comes easy. So there will be hurdles to overcome. Satan has a host of fiery darts that he aims at the ministry marriage. If the enemy can take out a clergy marriage, he gets a few more with it from the pews, as a bonus. So there are certainly more of those fiery darts thrown at the leader and his bride.

However, this exceptional marriage team boldly accept the challenges of marriage in ministry. And they willingly put in the work. Their goal: To give God every bit of the glory.

When God created man, He said it was not good for the man to be alone. So He created a teammate, a partner to come along beside the man. The Lord gave **"them"** instruction. They had the loving assignment to become one. She was to help him lead and have dominion with him.

God views everything in light of a team. God himself is a team of one: Father, Son, and Holy Spirit. So the extraordinary leader's marriage is a team of oneness: God, husband, and wife.

Marriage was created even before the church was born. Leaders have to grasp the concept that their marriage has priority over the ministry. It is religious to think otherwise. No wife should be neglected for the sake of the church. A man's bride is his first priority and ministry. His first assignment from God is to love and cherish her, provide for her and protect her. He lays down his life for her just as Christ did for his bride. If we see this snapshot of Christ's love throughout pulpits all over the world, we would make a powerful impact for the kingdom.

People need to see and want to see a love that lasts. They want to see leaders and their spouses living in love. They don't want to hear one thing over the pulpit and see something different outside. It breaks the heart of the church to see their pastors' marriage break apart (even if they contributed to it). When the pulpit marriage is thriving, it gives hope to the congregation for their own relationships.

The charge from God is a serious one - love like Christ did. The best sermon a leader can ever preach to his congregation is the one he lives in front of them. So his most effective marriage ministry is the way he treats his wife. Our marriages are a reflection of our relationship with God. If a leader is going to teach any part of that Bible, he had better be living it. No one wants to hear the message of a hypocrite.

Husbands, love your wives, just as Christ loved the church and gave himself up for her. Ephesians 5:25

How does one love like Christ? Be committed. God doesn't divorce the church. He never gives up on us. His love never fails. We deserved for him to quit on us. But He didn't and He doesn't. Aren't we glad about that? He is married to the backslider. So we should not quit on one another. We must eliminate divorce as an option. When we do, we will work harder to make our unions work. Therefore ensuring a higher rate of success.

He gave himself up for her. Christ did not have a common love for his bride. His love is extraordinary. He loved her with all of himself. Her name was inscribed on his hands. He held her close to his heart. He yearned for her to return his affection. But he never waited for her to earn it or to start acting right. She was 100% guilty in her rejection of him. But he laid down his life for hers. Her life was dearer to him than his own. She shunned him but he continued to pursue her. And at the end He rescues her.

Our God has modeled to us how we ought to love. We have a duty to model it to others. All impossible things become possible through our dependence on Christ. It's God's word that gives us the blueprint for how to make marriage work. We simply have to follow it.

Live joyfully with the wife of your youth. Ecclesiastes 9:9 shouts.

If we are going to be the church that Christ calls us to be then we have to do all that it will take to make our marriages work.

- The spouses date every week or nearly every week. This allows them to keep their love alive and to keep each other up on their priority list. All relationships require the investment of time. So it's this time of dating each other that they set aside all appointments to focus on one another.

- They meet weekly to discuss challenges that arise in the marriage. This husband-wife meeting strengthens their communication skills. They come to the meeting with the hope of resolution. They understand that yelling and silent treatment are unproductive and dishonoring to God. They attack the issues and not each other. They are committed to leave the meeting with answers. So they show each other respect. Besides they want to exemplify the behavior that they ask their congregants to follow.

➢ They cover each other. They know where their loyalty lies. They will not allow anyone to attack, put down, or harm the other in anyway. They don't air their business in church, social media, or anywhere in public view. An assault on one is an assault on the other. Proverbs 12:6

They do not counsel the opposite gender without the other present. They are proactive about their protection.

➢ They don't hold on to offenses. Offences will come but they forgive each other every day because they understand 2 things: 1) You can't move forward in your marriage without forgiveness. You will get stuck in anger and negativity. 2. You can't get forgiveness from God if you don't extend it to your spouse. So it is a gift they give to themselves and their mates. Ephesians 4:26

➢ They go away on vacations together. It is highly important that marriages are strengthened with time alone. This is not just the family vacation but weekend excursions and a weeklong getaway to keep the passion alive in their relationship. They refuse to neglect their marriage for the sake of the church. They understand that is simply a lack of faith.

➢ They parent as a team. Their children are not able to manipulate them or play them against one another.

They discuss in private how they will move forward in their team parenting. Then they execute their plan.

➢ They pray together. They recognize God as the main cord of their relationship. They pray in both good times and bad, trusting God to lead them.

The clergy marriage has to be able to stand the weight of ministry. It must be strong before the leader ever steps out to lead a congregation of people. He should not take on ministry if his marriage is weak. Leading a ministry is a heavy weight. If you put it on top of a weak marriage, the marriage will collapse and crumble. However a strong marriage has the capability of strengthening the ministry.

Paul makes it plain as he writes to Timothy, his son in the gospel. He instructs him that this is a requirement of leadership:

One that rules well his own house, having his children in subjection with all gravity; (For if a man know not how to rule his own house, how shall he take care of the church of God? I Timothy 3:4,5

We really don't take this scripture as seriously as we should. This is a solemn charge. Ruling your house well means loving your spouse and children and leading them according to scripture. Your family is your first ministry outside of your relationship to the Lord. Ruling one's house well means we should set a godly example for others to follow.

A wise pastor harnesses the strength of his marriage to help the ministry. It doesn't make much sense for a pastor to have a wife, then silence her when it comes to the church.

If you are one in your relationship, it aids the congregants to see the two as one. A ministry is more well-rounded when both husband and wife work together as a team.

It takes the two operating as one to be effective. Pastors are like spiritual parents to those they serve. And God's best is that children would have both a mother and a father. The entire image of God is displayed when you have both husband and wife leading in harmony.

Most congregations are comprised of majority women. So if you have a wife, it is imperative to have her on your team. There is much she will need to say. Include her. Listen to her admonitions and creative ideas. Do not dismiss her or ignore her for the applause of the church. She will make you better.

The enemy hates agreement in Christ. He hates oneness in righteousness. When making an important decision in your ministry, **always** involve your spouse. She is not just a teammate in marriage but she is also part of the ministry team. She wants what is in the best interest of the ministry. It can be detrimental to not include her. How much she is involved should be to the level you both agree. That will be different for every church. However she should never be silenced or excluded from the ministry.

In Genesis, God said that it was not good for the man to be alone. And so he created a wife for man as a suitable helper. It is the foolish leader who doesn't listen to his wife - acting as if he is alone and ignoring his wife's input.

Take a look at Pilate as he had to bring Jesus to judgment. Matt 27:19 God did not speak directly to Pilate. He spoke to his wife through a dream. And Pilate obeyed her. And it was in his best interest. Take note, Pilate was the one in authority, but God saw them as a team. And Pilate was wise enough to submit to his wife's counsel even though he was the government leader and not she.

In another passage of scripture, Genesis 21:12 Sarah told Abram to send Hagar away and God told Abram to obey what Sarah has said.

But God told Abraham, "Do not be upset over the boy and your servant. **Do whatever Sarah tells you***, for Isaac is the son through whom your descendants will be counted.* NLT

God is so wise. He created a team on purpose. There are many benefits to the team. The spouse is the closest person to the leader. The pastor's wife is able to see his flaws. She is the one who can say this is not right or we need to really pray about that. She helps the man of God. Many leaders get caught up in the applause of the congregation. Because he has shut down his wife as his teammate by not taking heed to her advice, the pastor can find himself in moral failure and out of the will of God.

Wives are able to spot Jezebel and any other seducing spirits well before their husbands. If she warns him, he ought to listen – even if he doesn't see it. Women know women in the same way men know men. The leader's wife is able to detect if a woman's motives are not pure. Many times, the leader is blinded by gifts, flattery, or the neediness of this spirit sent to relieve him of his anointing.

Some men have lost their ministries because they would not listen to their wives. Pride caused their hearts to swell where they could no longer hear her. The result is always tragic.

The same wisdom applies for the female pastor. It must be a team effort. Your husband is a vital member of the leadership team. However the female pastor has to learn to operate at another level of submission. While she may lead the ministry, she is still a wife and must submit to her husband. She must be wise enough to balance both roles. God 's design is the one to follow. The church will be deficient when both spouses are not involved in the ministry.

Do ministry as a team. Consider what your spouse is saying. Pray together about the ministry. Schedule a meeting about the ministry periodically with only the two of you present. This meeting is exclusive of board members and deacons. Once the two of you have heard from God, then you come on one accord to the meeting with board members. You will have great success.

The reward for such strenuous work is an exceptional marriage. It's a well-oiled machine. It works. It's not perfect, but it purrs. Where one is weak, the other puts forth their strength. Love covers their sins and mess-ups. And they keep loving for a lifetime. Others look and say, we can do it, too.

~Five~

The Heart of Ministry

In the past 10 years or so, clergy offices have taken a real beating. We have been blasted all over media as lacking integrity. Headlines have read:

> Victims Testify Bishop Molested Them
>
> Drugs Reportedly Found on Preacher
>
> Mega Church Founding Pastors Seek Divorce.
>
> Pastor Pleads Guilty in Embezzlement Case.
>
> Wife stabs preacher over affair

It is shameful and brings a reproach on the church and the name of our Lord. If we do not have integrity, we have nothing. What is integrity? It is soundness of moral character: the state of being whole and undivided. Integrity is being one with ourselves. It's when what we say and what we do are congruent. Integrity is the distinguishing characteristic of an exceptional leader. It is the only way that we can justly claim to be connected to God. It necessitates that we live a life above reproach.

> *The integrity of the upright shall guide them: but the perverseness of transgressors shall destroy them.*
> *(Proverb 11:3)*

It is the guiding force of our ministries. So how do leaders stray away from their moral compass? It all begins with their heart condition. In order to lead the way God intended, we must first understand that our ministry is no greater than our personal walk with God. Whatever issues that I allow to fester in my soul will be played out in my church. So, we must look to God to lead us and guide in those areas. We can never get comfortable with who we are to the degree that we stop working on ourselves.

> In Jeremiah 17:9 it reads, The heart *is* deceitful above all *things*, and desperately wicked: who can know it.

We cannot trust ourselves with our own heart, we must continually seek God, and put our hearts in his hands so that our motives will remain pure.

> Watch over your heart with all diligence, for from it flows the springs of life. Proverbs 4:23

One of the biggest mistakes leaders make is allowing the ugliness of sin to invade their hearts (bitterness, pride, lust, rejection, offence, etc.) If men or women of God are not working on themselves, they allow the flesh to lead them instead of the spirit of God and integrity is breached. There are many ways we compromise our character.

Pride seeps in.

Our charge is to lead the people to the Lord and not to ourselves. Some leaders get captivated by the glamour and glory of the ministry and want to take some for themselves. This is extremely dangerous. Jesus died for His church. He will not share that glory with another. If a leader is self-important, his pride will deplete him of every ounce of integrity.

Pride is often the brittle killer of ministries. When our focus is shifted from building God's kingdom according to His word to building a kingdom to ourselves, we are in trouble. Pride is able to dismantle our ministry piece by piece.

A prideful leader gets enamored with himself, thinking of himself more highly than he ought. He may have experienced a huge amount of success. After a while, he feels he can do whatever he wants and without repercussions. This happened to King David. He stayed home at a time when kings went to war. As a result, he fell into sexual sin with Bathsheba and then killed her husband to cover his sin. His lapse of integrity cost him much more than he wanted to pay. Thankfully he recovered. His story was written so that we would not err in the same way.

Sometimes a leader thinks so much of himself that he puts himself above the people. He gives orders and mete out commands while refusing himself to do what he asks of others. It is hypocritical to require the people to do something that we ourselves are not willing to do. We have witnessed leaders who require their congregations to fast while they never turn down their plates; even mandating that the "intercessors" pray and the congregation never has the opportunity to observe their own leader in prayer.

Some leaders are too busy and too important to attend the worship part of the service; while the congregation is encouraged to participate. What we do speaks volumes over what we say. We dismiss the significance of worship, when we ourselves opt out.

An ungodly leader is one who lacks integrity. She/he may preach integrity but never practice it. The people follow him or her because of charisma, not to be mistaken for the anointing. This type of leader is able to charm the people. But he can never truly lead them to Christ.

There are also some that get caught up in the money trap. It is unhealthy and ungodly to pursue money. Even those who start out with an honest heart can find themselves chasing dollars.

Seek ye first the kingdom of God and His righteousness and all these things will be added. Matthew 6:33

Ministry involves a life of sacrifice. Leaders have to learn to trust the Lord for their provision in the same way as laity. Every leader will be challenged financially in some way to believe God. It becomes more of a challenge, when there are so many needs and the people don't give as they should. A leader can become frustrated and shift their focus to money. When we learn to look to God for provision and not the people, we retain our integrity.

The Spirit of Rejection

It is easy to take on the spirit of rejection when negative events occur. There are many personalities that comprise the ministry. People come with all kinds of baggage. Many of them are rejected themselves. And rejected people reject others. So there is a group that will speak ill of the ministry and the leader. They did it to Jesus. If we follow Him, then we are due the same treatment. There will be some who throw fits when they don't get their way. There is another group who may think they are more qualified than you and should be in charge. And those who will just out and out buck your authority. No matter what happens you will find someone who is not happy with the decisions you make.

Extraordinary leaders don't hate the haters. In fact, God says quite the opposite.

But I say to you who hear, love your enemies, do good to those who hate you, bless those who curse you, pray for those who mistreat you. "Whoever hits you on the cheek, offer him the other also; and whoever takes away your coat, do not withhold your shirt from him. St Luke 6:27-29

It is also never appropriate to use God's holy pulpit to call out those who oppress you. Character requires that you do not retaliate. Do not render evil for evil. Love bears all things and is slow to anger.

Certainly you will feel the pain of the darts thrown at you. We are not immune to pain. However we take all wounds to the Chief Physician. Let him be our Healer. It is true that hurt people hurt people. So it is imperative that we guard our hearts with all diligence. Lest we become just like our offender.

Of course, none of this means that you must sit passively by and let wounded people dismantle the ministry. We confront those who are in error. We are to first try to handle it one on one. Then we bring them in with other believers. Finally there is a time to bring them before the congregation.

St. Matthew 18:15-17 "If a brother sins against you, go to him privately and confront him with his fault. If he listens and confesses it, you have won back a brother. ¹⁶ But if not, then take one or two others with you and go back to him again, proving everything you say by these witnesses. ¹⁷ If he still refuses to listen, then take your case to the church, and if the church's verdict favors you, but he won't accept it, then the church should excommunicate him.[a]

Low Self-image

Godly confidence keeps our integrity intact. Be confident in who you are in Christ. A low self-image will cause a leader to be jealous, competitive, and controlling. If a leader is unsure of himself, he will use and/or abuse the people to fulfill some lack in his own life. He will yearn for affirmation and acceptance. Because of his insecurity, he will do anything to get applause. The leader who loses his identity takes no issue with compromising the gospel. If giving in settles some need in his life, he will do it.

We must know that our image is to be met in Jesus Christ alone. So even if there are times of struggle, we can march ourselves back to the word, allowing God to repair any holes.

Bitterness

The wisdom of God dissuades us from giving our hearts totally to the church. That position is only reserved for the Lord. If a leader does make that mistake, he is setting himself up for hurt and rejection. Giving your heart to the church means you are giving it to an unstable, vacillating people. This is a guarantee that eventually your heart will be broken. We must give our hearts totally to God, not to people or we will end up discouraged.

Discouragement causes us to look at God at a slant. Eventually we blame Him for our pain; because he is the one who called us to this work. This pushes us further away from God and puts our character at stake.

If we don't have anyone close to us to help us navigate through those feelings, we can become bitter. All of this bitterness can settle in the heart as we continue to preach and lead God's people. The result is a hard heart, which leads us away from God.

One trigger for this is when people leave the ministry. And please believe, they WILL leave your church. Some will leave with your blessing but some will not. Either way, don't take it personally; no matter how personal they try to make it. People come and go. That's just the way ministry works. But don't let them take a piece of your heart with them.

Allow them to leave with your heart and the doors open for their return. Release them (never beg anyone to stay). If they don't want to be there, you really don't want them there. But understand they may return sometime down the line in another season. But even if they don't. Be okay with it. You only want to lead those that believe God has set you in their lives. Otherwise you may find yourself casting pearls.

The best response when a member leaves, is to give it totally to the Lord. It may sting a little. But ultimately they are God's people. They should only enter and exit the ministry when he calls. If a sheep is leaving the fold prematurely, gracefully release him. Trust them in the hands of the Chief Shepherd but always leave the door open for their return.

There are a few extreme cases where you would not allow a member to return. But those are exceptions, not the rule. Seek godly counsel and be led by the spirit of God.

Well Balanced

We must embrace and operate in a spirit of excellence. Joseph was a man of character. With all the suffering Joseph endured, he never lost his integrity. No matter what he faced, the Bible said that God was with Joseph. That's what we want in our ministries - God with us at all times. This requires that we preach in word and deed - truth covered in grace.

Truth without grace leaves one self-righteous and legalistic. Grace without truth promotes compromise and is a measure of false compassion. We must blend these two qualities into our personal life, mimicking the character of Christ. We are to govern ourselves in a way that promotes holiness. In a loving atmosphere, we must embrace a holy unchangeable high standard. This is not easy to do. Most people are at one end of the spectrum or the other. Our Gracious God requires the merging of the two virtues in order that we would love completely. It is the rare individual who can balance standing in truth from a graceful perspective. It's the balance that Jesus demonstrated in being both the Lion of Judah and the Lamb of God.

Grace without truth will spoil us and truth without grace will harm us. Either end of the scale will keep us stymied in religion.

Promoting truth without grace lends us an uneven hand even when applied to ourselves. It is not honorable to be overly critical of yourself. Because if you are unable to receive the grace of God for your life, you certainly will not give it to others. And if you allow yourself only a diet of grace, you will find yourself and those you lead, castaways.

A spirit of excellence keeps us balanced and keeps our character in check.

The Answer

Exceptional leaders have a duty to lead *themselves* to God. There must be a time of pulling away and sitting in the presence of God. When we take time to speak to God and hear from Him, we are strengthened and receive the direction we need. This requires that we give attention to studying the word of God, not just to present a sermon but to feed our spirit man for growth and development.

Study to show thyself approved unto God, a workman that needed not to be ashamed, rightly dividing the word of truth. II Timothy 2:15

Ordination and licensing do not serve as proof that a leader has arrived. We need to continue to grow spiritually. Our faith needs to increase. Faith comes by hearing the word of God. The extraordinary leader not only studies the word himself but he also listens to other ministers' messages to **receive** (not to re-preach their sermons).

When clergy is at risk, the answer is to seek help. The fear of what people will say or how it will look is a hindrance to many leaders. Pastors are real people with real issues: financial challenges, marital struggles, family drama, and more. Some leaders may even struggle with depression. Unfortunately they often think they must keep up a certain image for the sake of the ministry. So they suffer silently.

There is so much help is available. None of us is infallible. Only God is. We must seek out the help that we need to continue with the call of God on our lives. Marriage counseling and pastoral accountability can be the lifeline to a leader in trouble. We just have to be humble enough to seek it out.

    Integrity is at the crux of the successful ministry. Without it, we are exempted from inheriting the Kingdom of God. Integrity will get us where we need to go. Be extraordinary. Let us hold to our Christian values and live like God is always watching. **Because He is.**

The eyes of the Lord are in every place, beholding the evil and the good. Proverbs 15:3

~Six~

Accountability

And let us consider how we may spur one another on toward love and good deeds. Let us not give up meeting together, as some are in the habit of doing, but let us encourage one another—and all the more as you see the day approaching. Hebrews 10:25

Emily Dennis is the first lady of St. John's Hypothetical Church. She was flipping through her husband's phone looking at some pics when she stumbled upon some pornography. She was shocked. She felt hurt and betrayed. After she confronted her husband, she went straight to the Council. The Council is composed of 5 leaders that have agreed to hold each other accountable.

The Council stepped in right away. They were discrete in not exposing the Pastor to his congregation. But put in safeguards to keep him from falling again. He was asked to step down from ministering for a short season to focus in on healing for himself and his family. His accountability plan included ongoing prayer, individual counseling and marriage counseling for himself and his wife, help with managing the ministry, and a subscription to Covenant Eyes, an internet filtering and accountability program that tracks visits to pornography sites and sends the report to the designated person.

The couple worked through their issues and was healed and restored. The Pastor is still respected and the ministry is thriving and healthy today. This is ideally what happens when there is a culture of accountability in place.

Certainly we all agree that a ministry leader is ultimately accountable to the Lord. But earthly accountability is also very crucial to clergy. A pastor who doesn't have anyone to answer to can easily find himself with an inflated ego. And pride can cause him to have blind spots which block his ability to see and sense danger. Accountability guards against this.

However the ministry leader must be willing to participate in consistent and honest communication with trustworthy persons. These meetings should be conducted in an air of love and gentleness. The spirit of accountability should be consistent with Galatians 6:1, "Brothers, if anyone is caught in any transgression, you who are spiritual should restore him in a spirit of gentleness, Keep watch on yourself, lest you too be tempted." In light of this scripture, it insists that our approach be merciful.

Nevertheless the leader must honestly and sincerely submit to those who are in position.

An exceptional leader will surround himself with wise counsel. I John 1:8-10 reminds us why we need accountability:

If we claim to be without sin, we deceive ourselves and the truth is not in us. If we confess our sins, he is faithful and just and will forgive us our sins and purify us from all unrighteousness. If we claim we have not sinned, we make him out to be a liar and his word is not in us.

Accountability in all fields build trust with those you lead, this is especially true in ministry.

In the multitude of counselors there is safety. Proverbs. 11:14

The right accountability team can serve as protection from congregations who under protect their leader and those who over-protect their shepherd. It saves leaders from harming themselves and others. Unfortunately many leaders fear being held accountable and so they hide from it. Hiding from it can be detrimental to the ministry.

We are called to be in community with one another. It is improper to think that we can operate independently from the body of believers. We are all members of the same body. We are fitly joined together. Accountability is about sharing our lives in an intimate way with others. We are helpers one of another. We walk beside our brothers and sisters not in condemnation but always in hope of reconciliation.

It takes self-discipline to set personal boundaries that protect against as the scripture says, "even the appearance of impropriety". Certain restrictions should be set in place. For example, male pastors should not counsel females privately neither should female pastors counsel males privately. Pastors should not exclusively handle ministry funds. There must be persons in place to oversee and limit access. This doesn't just protect the church but it also protects the leader against false accusations.

Certainly as leaders, we get to select to whom we will submit. Wisdom will cause you to choose those who are exemplary in their own lives. You want those who are living lives above reproach. Of course, they do not have to be perfect, but living without compromise.

Proper accountability is void of control, manipulation, or coercion. It is a voluntary surrender of our right to live outside of God's law. So we enlist those who will walk beside us to support, encourage, teach, and disciple.

No man is an island. God designed it so that we would need and rely on each other. The foolish say, "I need no one." The exceptional pastor understands the need for accountability and welcomes it.

~Seven~
Personal & Church Finances

Faithful stewardship is required of those called to lead. We must be conscious of where all of God's money is distributed. We cannot take lightly the handling of all that belongs to Him.

Wherever a leader is strong, that's where the church will be strong. Conversely, wherever he is weak, it will show up in his ministry. If you do not manage your own finances well, then it is probable that you will not be a good manager of the church's finances.

Most pastors struggle in their personal finances because they just haven't had proper training. Unfortunately, there will not be much difference in the way they handle the church finances. They will apply the same skill set.

If you financial management is not your strong suit, pull on that gift in someone else in the ministry. If you cannot find someone skilled and trustworthy enough, pay a professional. He can get the job done. When we are ignorant in an area, we tend to overestimate the costs and underestimate the value. A professional's charges depend on the amount of activity needed. The costs are often much smaller than anticipated. It is worth it to make sure the finances are being handled properly. It is a requirement of God.

> I Corinthians 4:2 Now it is required that those who have been given a trust must prove faithful.

Often ministries feel hard hit for finances because people are challenged in their giving. It has been said when people join a ministry their money is the last to come. And when they leave, it's the first to go. If people don't like something said or done by the leader, they may withdraw or cutback on giving. Others are just poor stewards and spend more than they earn. They do not fully understand the value of tithing.

The Lord designed that the church should be supported by the tithes and offerings. Most churches receive less than 10% of the income it should be operating on. So we really have to make good use of all that we receive. That means operating below your income. Our monthly expenses should not exceed the church's monthly collection. If we find ourselves in the red, we will need to scale back.

It is not wise for the ministry leader to spend more than what comes in. He may have a grand vision for a ministry with only a few members who bring in a small income to the church. It is not wise for him to spend the church assets to purchase a property that the congregation is unable to sustain. It is not faith, but poor stewardship.

There have been many pastors who lost their ministries because they had grandiose dreams and visions with modest means. There has to be a place for wisdom in the way we run God's ministries. It is unwise to run ahead of the vision. God will let us know when He is asking us to make a big faith move. But we have to listen clearly and wholly.

We can't get part of the vision and run into action. We must make sure that we are moving in the timing of God. That requires that we exercise patience. We can get excited and passionate about the work we are called to do, but we must allow patience to have her perfect work in our lives. It is reckless to receive a word from God regarding the vision, but violate all of His precepts in the process.

Joseph's dream took more than 20 years to come to pass. Just because God gives you a vision it doesn't mean it's to happen in this season. We must wait for the timing of God. The revelation is that, **You can never force a vision to come to pass before its time.**

The blessing of the unusual church is that she operates debt-free. Because the leader prayerfully considers the will of God over the will of the people in decision making. Even if a ministry doesn't start out debt-free, it should be the aim. The outstanding leader will execute a plan that takes the ministry in that direction.

God will give us the provision for the vision. The best objective is to make cash purchases and avoid debt as much as possible. If you can't afford to pay cash for a purchase, wait until you can. Certainly there is an exception in purchasing a building. However we still want to make sure that it is affordable and we have a plan in place to cancel the debt. However credit cards and loans are not God's best for us. Debt is not a blessing; but a curse. The church should not position itself as a borrower. The promise of God is that we would be lenders.

We must remember that the borrower is servant to the lender. Our position as the bride of Christ demands that we resist the offer to be entangled in debt. We must work to eliminate debt from our financial portfolios.

TITHES & OFFERINGS

When we offer tithes and offerings to God, it is a symbol of our love and trust. Many leaders do not always pay tithes. They have not quite grasped the revelation of tithing.

Because there are so many needs, generally leaders give benevolently all of the time. The excellent leader, however, does not count his benevolence (which is an offering) towards his tithes. He puts into action the principles he teaches to his congregation. The tithe is holy unto the Lord.

The exceptional leader pays tithes personally and a tithe of all that the ministry receives is also offered back to God. The tithe represents that God is first. When the Lord is recognized first in our giving, He blesses us. So just as we do with our personal finances, so should every ministry offer a tithe back to God.

Pray that the finances that the Lord has for your ministry will be released and not one dime of it held back. And then teach the people about giving. This is the only way that people will be blessed. Don't concern yourself with what they may think. Obey God. Teach without inhibition.

Never manipulate or put an overemphasis on giving. There must be balance. Teach God's people to tithe and to give. Don't coerce them or guilt them into it. Trust God to touch the hearts of His people. Schemes and gimmicks grieve the Holy Spirit and often backfire. God's people should not be subjected to such witchcraft...in the church.

People have to grow into giving. Just like they have to mature into other spiritual virtues. They must learn that it is a privilege to give. The scripture says that it is more blessed to give than to receive. So to stand in the place of the giver is the most prosperous place. This concept is often reached in maturity.

Traditional shepherds tend to get angry with the congregants for their lack of giving. They may yell and belittle the sheep Because there are so many needs, generally leaders give benevolently all of the time. The excellent leader, however, does not count his benevolence (which is an offering) towards his tithes. He puts into action the principles he teaches to his congregation. The tithe is holy unto the Lord.

Some members are personally harassed. Leaders have been known to chase the tithe down. This shows a lack of trust for God to provide. That leader is looking to the people for provision. But he really can't expect them to trust God if he doesn't. The people will follow their leader.

Giving is the avenue that God has given for the church to grow. So of course, the extraordinary pastor is a giver. He demonstrates His belief and trust in God through tithing. The unusual pastor doesn't skimp or skip the tithe. He gives God what is due Him. He doesn't justify his tithe away because of his meager income or other gifts given to others.

He still maintains his covenant by tithing off all increase that comes his way personally and corporately.

A ministry/church that tithes will see God's hand in their finances. Tithing is trusting in God. Tithing is our way of saying Lord you are primary. So even as we expect Christian businesses to tithe, so ought the ministry/church to tithe as a corporate body. The tithe is cyclical in nature. It doesn't end or stop at one particular ministry. It continues to flow through the body and throughout God's kingdom.

Module A: Suzy Favor gives her 10% to Treetop Baptist. If Treetop is not a tithing ministry it stops here.

However if Treetop is an unusual ministry that really believes in the principle of tithing, the process is different.

Module B: Suzy Favor gives her 10% to Treetop Baptist. Treetop gives a tenth to a new ministry, The Gathering. The Gathering gives a tenth to Go Tell It Ministries, Go Tell It gives a tenth to Body of Believers Church…and so on and so on.

Which module do you think God designed? Our Great King is a multiplier. So module B is what the unusual church embraces.

SAVINGS

Savings is a principle encouraged by scripture. The unusual leader personally saves first for his/her family from his/her own salary. After tithes and offerings, 10% is put away (whether he thinks he can afford it or not). He will find that he can't afford NOT to save.

He sets up a short term savings account for emergencies. This account caps at no less than $1000. The long term savings account has about 8 months' worth of living expenses. This will help to sustain the clergy family in case of church splits, job terminations, sickness, etc.

A vacation account is also set up in case that the ministry is unable to pay for vacations. Vacations are a necessity and not an option in this profession. Ministry can be very stressful. In order to combat that stress, it is suggested that clergy get away once every quarter. Realistically, that means we have to save for it. So establish a vacation account and add to it every week.

Any other savings accounts and investments he wants to set up are certainly a plus. However they are established only after the short term and long term accounts. He adds on other accounts as the Lord leads.

In the same way, the exceptional leader sets these things up for himself, he should also set up the unusual *church* with savings accounts.

In the colder states, church attendance usually drops during the summer months. A rainy day account can be set up for such times. Churches should have other savings accounts as well: outreach, building projects, sound equipment, special events, etc.

If you are not sure how to do this. Take 10% of the weekly collection and deposit into the church's savings accounts. Distribute that 10% over the various savings accounts. It may seem like a drop in a bucket. But know if you keep dropping that bucket will eventually fill up.

Many churches/ministries do not have savings accounts.

They are constantly taking from the general fund, and keep finding themselves struggling and coming up short. Therefore they will always have to go to the people to cover shortfalls. Unusual churches are wise. They plan and save to cover future costs.

INVESTMENTS

Pastors have a duty to establish an IRA for his retirement needs. Stocks, bonds, annuities, mutual funds, etc. are different types of investment vehicles. He takes time to pray and seek the Lord's counsel. It's the Lord's money and He knows how to multiply it. Too often traditional clergy and their families have no retirement or life insurance. After many years of service, they are left with nothing. The excellent leader is covered. He has sought the Lord for a plan.

> He that handles a matter wisely shall find good: and whoso trusteth in the LORD, happy is he. Proverbs 16:20

There is wisdom for every situation we face. As you set up investments for your future, the church should also have investments. Clergy should seek the Lord about how to invest the churches money for kingdom purposes. Please understand that it is unethical to get caught up in get-rich-quick schemes and multi-level marketing ploys. It will take careful prayer and planning to research investing God's money. Even if it's something as modest as a certificate of deposit or money market certificate, time should be given to prayer.

In St. Matthew 25: 14-30, it reads

¹⁴ "Again, it will be like a man going on a journey, who called his servants and entrusted his wealth to them. ¹⁵ To one he gave five bags of gold, to another two bags, and to another one bag,[a] each according to his ability. Then he went on his journey. ¹⁶ The man who had received five bags of gold went at once and put his money to work and gained five bags more. ¹⁷ So also, the one with two bags of gold gained two more. ¹⁸ But the man who had received one bag went off, dug a hole in the ground and hid his master's money.

¹⁹ "After a long time the master of those servants returned and settled accounts with them. ²⁰ The man who had received five bags of gold brought the other five. 'Master,' he said, 'you entrusted me with five bags of gold. See, I have gained five more.'

²¹ "His master replied, 'Well done, good and faithful servant! You have been faithful with a few things; I will put you in charge of many things. Come and share your master's happiness!' ²² "The man with two bags of gold also came. 'Master,' he said, 'you entrusted me with two bags of gold; see, I have gained two more.' ²³ "His master replied, 'Well done, good and faithful servant! You have been faithful with a few things; I will put you in charge of many things. Come and share your master's happiness!'

²⁴ "Then the man who had received one bag of gold came. 'Master,' he said, 'I knew that you are a hard man, harvesting where you have not sown and gathering where you have not scattered seed. ²⁵ So I was afraid and went out and hid your gold in the ground. See, here is what belongs to you.' ²⁶ "His master replied, 'You wicked, lazy servant! So you knew that I harvest where I have not sown and gather where I have not scattered seed? ²⁷ Well then, you should have put my money on deposit with the bankers, so that when I

returned I would have received it back with interest. [28] "'So take the bag of gold from him and give it to the one who has ten bags. [29] For whoever has will be given more, and they will have an abundance. Whoever does not have, even what they have will be taken from them. [30] And throw that worthless servant outside, into the darkness, where there will be weeping and gnashing of teeth.'

We can see that investments are a biblical principle. Our faithful Lord gives seed to the sower. He expects us to increase what he has given us. And He only trusts those who trust Him.

~Eight~

Burning or Burnout?

Come away to a deserted place all by yourselves and rest a while. ~Mark 6:31

Over the past 10 years or so, we have witnessed an anomaly. Pastors have committed suicide at an alarming rate. Somehow these men and women were so lost in the ministry that they were empty of faith. If faith is lost, there is no hope. When the man or woman of God is hopeless, what hope is there for those that they lead?

We start out passionate and on fire for God and end up distant from God, despising the ministry. There are many reasons why leaders lose their fervor for ministry. The most important one is due to lack of self-care.

For the first years of our lives, it was the responsibility of our parents to take care of us. God gave them the assignment until we were old enough to take care of ourselves. And then they passed the baton. Unfortunately we dropped the baton. Leaders do a terrible job of caring for themselves. We see it as almost honorable to neglect our own care for the care of others.

Somewhere along the way, we've received messages that told us that it was selfish to take care of ourselves. And so as leaders yearning for righteousness, we abandoned care of ourselves. Some of us mistakenly think that it is up to God to care for us as we rush around caring for others.

We have to understand that God gives that holy assignment to us. We are to give attention and thought to caring for ourselves. It is an assignment of stewardship given to us by a Holy and Loving God.

Matthew 22:37-38 says, Love God with all of your heart, soul, strength and mind and love your neighbor as yourself. That statement is a command to love three: God, yourself and your neighbor. And in that order. The wisdom is that we would love ourselves. Therefore we are able to love our neighbor.

I Corinthians 6:19-20 reads, Do you not know that your bodies are the temples of the Holy Spirit, who is in you, whom you have received from God? You are not your own; You were bought at a price. **Therefore honor God with your bodies.** (emphasis ours)

Is God honored in the way that you take care of you? Many leaders are operating on very little sleep, rising early and going to bed late.

Proverbs 1:27 says, It is vain for you to rise up early, to sit up late, to eat the bread of sorrow: for so he giveth his beloved sleep.

For some reason we give ourselves a pass. and then

wonder why we are so tired.

> Ecclesiastes 5:12 The sleep of a laborer is sweet.

Why must a ministry leader get adequate sleep? Sleep has many benefits. A good night's sleep improves our memory, our mood, decision-making, creativity, and focus. We really cannot afford to skip sleep. We need all of those benefits for effective leadership.

> Romans 12:1 says Therefore I urge you brothers and sisters, in view of God's mercy, to offer your bodies as a living sacrifice holy and pleasing to God, this is your true and proper worship.

If we are offering our bodies as a sacrifice does God receive it? In order to determine that we need to understand that God only accepts a worthy sacrifice. If your body is tired, worn, diseased, and wrecked with pain due to neglect, is it an acceptable sacrifice? Is He glorified in your sacrifice?

Busyness is a norm in our society. You can hardly go any length of time without hearing someone excuse themselves with their busyness. It is socially acceptable. That same message has leaked into the church. If you aren't busy than you really aren't productive. In fact, driven leaders are often applauded for their overexertion by their peers. Rarely is a leader rebuked for working too long or too hard, until he has suffered a heart attack or stroke or some other health condition.

The expectation is that the leader sacrifice everything for the ministry (eh hem…for God). So we over commit. We push. We work 24-7 with no days off. We drag our wearied bodies from one event to the other. We give until there's nothing left to give and then we try to give more. We are pushing and rushing at an impossible pace... Until we crash.

We go about with our busyness thinking God is pleased. And He still says the laborers are few.

According to the Schaeffer Institute, 70 percent of pastors constantly fight depression, and 71 percent are burned out. These are some staggering numbers. We read them and we just move on past them. Nothing shakes us to say, stop here and consider. We should pause for a minute and see the ploy of the enemy. Seventy percent is a large majority. Are you in either category or headed that way? Let's stop this cycle. Let's mean it when we say, "no more church as usual."

Presently there is little to no self-care of the average pastor. They don't take vitamins. They don't exercise. They are too busy to cook. So nutritious meals are at a deficient. They fill up on junky fast food. They don't rest. And they expect their bodies to keep up. They won't. They will eventually give out. This is why pastors have so many heart attacks and strokes.

It has been said if the enemy can't stop us, he pushes us. And that's what happens in burnout. The enemy pushes us further than God requires. We become unsettled in our spirits, overwhelmed and anxious. If we aren't careful, we will take on responsibilities that do not belong to us. And peace is lost.

When a leader approaches burnout, his thought patterns shift to human strength rather than God's strength. He finds himself discouraged. He will eventually find himself in a bitter place, complaining about the call he once considered a privilege. What a trap we have fallen into when we begin to blame our Loving Father for our tiredness.

Exodus 20::8 The Lord commands us to remember the Sabbath day to keep it holy. This Sabbath was created for us. If the God of all creation rested after speaking the world into existence, why do we exempt ourselves from rest? Are we too important to rest? Have we made ourselves more important than God? There has to be a place and time for respite.

If we are to avoid burnout, we must keep the Sabbath as God commanded. It is an act of self-care. Not as a *must do*, but as an intentional offering of the day and ourselves back to God.

The truth of the matter is that the labor will <u>never</u> get all done. Our life on earth is limited. We will leave some work for those who come behind us. And it is really okay.

As leaders who teach others to obey God, we must be first partakers of the fruit. He says to rest, therefore we ought to. God calls us to a life of peace and rest.

There must be a time to disengage from ministry. Ministry can be intense. We are not suggesting a vacation from God. You never need that. But you do need to avoid viewing God as a taskmaster, who is constantly requiring you to "do." Cut off the fountain of complaint that is turned on by over commitment. Our loving Lord calls you to Himself for intimacy and rest. He wants us to just "be". The exceptional leader acts like Mary and the unexceptional leader acts like Martha. Mary chose resting at the Lord's feet. Martha chose working for the Lord. And the scripture says Mary chose the good part.

The Sabbath is what keeps us all from burnout. It's time

spent with the Lord and away from the people and the tasks. It's an opportunity to slow down and take assessment of our own personal relationship with God, ourselves and others. It's a time to commune with Him. Let the fire of His presence replenish us. We all need it.

Poor self-care is a matter of wrong thought processes. Often leaders mistake self-care for selfishness. There is nothing selfish about taking proper care of yourself. How can you care for others if your own body is hindered? It's the same idea as securing your own oxygen mask first before assisting others. It's not a selfish act but selfless.

Self-care and selfishness both mean to care for oneself. However selfishness is only concerned with one's own benefit with no regard for anyone else (except that it might benefit). Self-care is concerned with your own benefit **and** the benefits of others. Self-care is a holy command from God that we would take care of ourselves so that we can properly and effectively serve Him and others.

Self-care means:

- Eating right. It helps keep us energized and maintain good health to avoid hypertension and other diseases.
- Drinking lots of water.
- Getting 6-8 hours of sleep per night
- Taking time out to honor the Sabbath. It helps us to recharge.
- Exercising. Walking, jogging or working out the gym aids in good health and raising our energy level.

Shouldn't we give God the best of us? Doesn't he deserve a healthy, energized, well-balanced servant? It takes self-discipline to administer self-care. It's not something we can do once or twice. It has to reflect the way we live every day. As we connect to God, we will find ourselves far more productive.

Every one of us ought to honor the Sabbath. It is not easy but certainly necessary. We cannot take the day we hold services as our Sabbath because it is a day of work. (Remember the Sabbath was made for man). Choose another day. This is the day that you will elect to NOT receive phone calls or engage in any type of church work. It is your time to sit at the master's feet. Perhaps do a media fast. Slow down.

For bi-vocational leaders, it may impossible for you to take a complete Sabbath. However you can be creative. Taking a Sabbath for you can mean setting aside 5+ hours after work to just do nothing. You can take Mondays (for example) after you leave your secular job, to rest. No ministry or work is allowed on your Sabbath. Sit at His feet. Let Him refresh you.

You have to know it's okay. The world and the church will go on without you. Jesus is the only Savior of the world. You are simply His servant.

Permission granted to take off your super hero cape.

Now chill.

~Nine~

Engaging The Congregation

The number 1 complaint of pastors is the lack of help in running the ministry. Why is it that pastors seem to have to do every task and be on every post when there are capable men and women in the ministry?

There are many reasons. Sometimes it's because leaders actually think no one else can do the jobs correctly. They may allow only one or two people to assist in the ministry. Or they complain that people aren't faithful enough. So they find themselves overworked and overwhelmed.

The truth is most people are willing to help in the ministry. It may mean that we have to restructure what we are asking them to do. Sometimes it means just breaking one job down into multiple pieces. Perhaps 3 persons can do a particular job instead of one. But it's going to always mean training. You cannot throw a congregant into any position and just expect them to know what to do. Extensive and ongoing training is necessary.

The key to success is to raise a leader and then require leaders to birth new leaders.

Former generations were taught in the church that leadership was only for a select few. Because of that small thinking, we did not reach our potential as the church.

The extraordinary leader shifts from this ineffective church model to one that Jesus employed. He had 12 followers and they were all leaders. Certainly they had different functions and duties. Nevertheless, He was able to impart his spirit and send them to lead the world to Himself. They turned the world upside down. Today, we have that same opportunity to turn the world topsy-turvy.

Our assignment is to raise up an army for Christ. Every arm of military service has several leaders: squad leaders, platoon leaders, captains, majors, lieutenants, colonels, majors, and generals. Each of these are leadership positions. There are several leaders within the military structure. And so is it with the body of Christ. In order for God's army of believers to be effective, extraordinary leaders will have to raise up and release more leaders in the kingdom.

The best strategy is to empower all men, young and old, to know and understand their true identity in Christ. Only then will they walk in their divine authority and compel others to follow them as they follow Christ.

The extraordinary pastor engages his youth. He realizes how valuable the next generation is to the longevity of the church. They bring another dynamic into the ministry. So he teaches the children to pray. He allows them to read scripture. He lets the babies hold the basket to collect the offering. They can be hosts and hostesses. They can work in the media ministry.

Start up a social media ministry and let the young people have at it. Let teens help teach children's church. Allow the little ones to dance on the dance team. Allow everyone the opportunity to use their gifts to worship the Lord.

It is equally encumbent upon outstanding leaders to release women of God to use their gifts, talents, and abilities to draw men and women to Christ. The Lord pours His spirit upon all flesh – our sons and daughters will prophesy. (Joel 2:28)

In past years, churches and their leaders discouraged women from using the very gifts that God gave them. They misinterpreted scripture to disqualify a majority of the church population. This is not the blueprint of a successful church.

Encourage women to use their gifts, talents, and abilities to serve. Train and push them to be all that God has intended. God created His daughters, not as an afterthought. He purposely gifted women and uses them greatly. He releases women to minister, prophesy, evangelize, etc. - in order to win the lost. We see a prime example in scripture where the woman at the well led an entire city to "Come see a man". (John 4)   God used women in the past. He uses women presently and He will continue to use His daughters for His Kingdom. Because the extraordinary leader agrees with God in regards to women in ministry, he will have far more available help than those who don't.

We must shift from the "usual" to an irregular church pattern. The usual just doesn't work. That means we must give birth to leaders who never even considered themselves as such.

Leaders can grow into whom they will become, if we will let them. Many may not be polished or skilled. If we are to move from old ineffective ideals of who can actually be a leader, it will mean that we consider that sometimes the leaders on our team will not be as knowledgeable as we would like. They may not come to us with degrees or licenses. Nevertheless there is a place for each one.

Jesus chose some pretty unusual characters to become leaders of the church. They were rough around the edges. Peter was rash and impetuous. Thomas struggled in his faith. James and John were prideful, arguing over who would sit in the best seat. And none of the disciples were really loyal except for John.

These outrageous gentlemen did not come into maturity until after Christ had ascended. They had some real issues. And the scripture describes some of them as "unlearned men". Most of us, would never have allowed them to be leaders. But God did. And they were successful.

God uses men and women who have a different slant. He uses those who think outside of the box. So let's not use the box to determine who can assist us in ministry. If we aren't counting people out, we will have a bigger pool to pull people from.

If we are to be exceptional, we must be able to duplicate ourselves. We cannot be intimidated by someone else's proficiency or stalled by someone's deficiency. We trust God with them all.

It is crucial to have someone in place that can do

everything that you do. If you are ever sick, have a family emergency or need to go on vacation, etc., you won't have to worry about the ministry. The unusual church is able to operate effectively without the leader's presence. It's God's church and it does not belong to one man. The ministry work is a collaborative effort. It must function as a whole body.

The old ineffective pastoral model was that the pastor did everything himself. The extraordinary model embraces the idea of team ministry. You need a team to do all that you are called to do. But you must trust God to give you that team. When he does, do not reject them at face value. Pour yourself into that team. Make sure that they have your spirit. Teach, train, and re-teach without being annoyed.

In order to produce a viable squad, it's going to require that you invest the time and energy to train them. Shift people around until you find exactly where they fit. You will be amazed at the results.

Be careful to not show respect of persons as you are preparing people to serve. There is a place for everyone to serve: cleaning the church, mowing the lawn, handling audio equipment, computer duties, passing out literature, teaching, counting money. The jobs may range from simple to complex. There is something everyone can do. So there is no need to rely on a few. Let's leave no member left behind.

Of course, every person won't help. However you can engage the majority of the congregation by creating opportunities for them to serve. Some will serve regularly. Some will only serve every now and then. You will need both sets of people to keep the ministry moving forward. So for those who do not want to make a regular commitment, give them isolated tasks. If you give them jobs like that, they will be more likely to participate.

Maybe some people will be able to donate items needed for a special event. Or maybe they can be a substitute for the cleaning crew once every quarter. There is more than one way for people to serve.

People have varying degrees of maturity levels, abilities and different life circumstances. Allow them to plug in whenever and wherever is best suitable for the ministry and the congregant. We cannot all fit into the same mold. Find what people "love" to do and put them in place, even if its temporary.

We can raise our level of ministry by using those that are least likely, those that others would disqualify. There are many treasures sitting idly in congregations all over the world because they have been discounted by some "average" leader. The exceptional leader looks for the good in others therefore he finds it. Everyone can serve in some capacity.

> Everything you need is in someone around you.
> ~Mike Murdock

God will not leave you operating at a deficit for human resources. If you are willing to train people, you will have who you need. Traditional leaders often feel they don't have the time to train. They want people to come to them already ready, willing, and able. Some will. But most will not. It is unreasonable to expect that everyone will come to you knowing exactly how to serve. Even in the simplest task, people will need to be trained in your way of doing it. And people are more confident in helping if they know that someone will show them how to help.

Additionally, do not limit yourself to those who are members. In our ministry, we have definitely been served by those who belong to mega-ministries and those who have no church home at all. Mega ministries have a host of talented people who will never get to sing on their church's praise team. Invite them to sing on yours every so often or for major events. The gifts are for the Kingdom of God. Invite them to share their gifts.

We also do not limit ourselves to the "saved". We also invite unbelievers to help us. When we are serving the homeless, we have saved and unsaved alike who pitch in to make sandwiches and prepare meals. People are generally willing to help. Let them. It's also a clever way to do inside-out evangelism, bringing them in through service.

Discover the gifts in your congregation then allow them to serve without micro managing. Let the creativity flow. Trust God to work what He needs to work in His people.

As a final note, every extraordinary leader should learn different ways to appreciate those who come beside him to assist in the ministry.

Gratitude always reaps great benefits. A little "thank you" can go a long way. The people are serving you because of their relationship with God; but don't dismiss what they bring. Average leaders think that's what they should do for God considering all He has done for them. While that is true, it is the wrong attitude.

Be appreciative. Offer a hand written note, a small gift, or public acknowledgment. Look for creative ways to bless the people that bless you. Don't take their service to God for granted. Everyone likes a little appreciation every now and then. Don't just wait for an annual event to show gratitude. A small token of recognition can do great things in encouraging the people in their service. When people feel appreciated, they will continue in their service.

The Leader's Library

Apostolic Foundations – Arthur Katz

Dangerous Surrender ~Kay Warren

Deep and Wide ~Andy Stanley

God's Big Idea – Dr. Myles Munroe

High Call High Privilege – Gail MacDonald

Maximized Manhood ~ Dr. Edwin Cole

The Pursuit of God ~ A. W. Tozer

Other Books By The Authors

A Woman's Place: Leading Ladies Speak Compiled by Crystal Jones & Joceline Bronson

Extreme Money Makeover by Oscar & Crystal Jones

Fast Food for the Married Soul by Oscar & Crystal Jones

Heart of the Roar by Oscar Jones

I Want A Husband, Too by Crystal Jones

LeaderShift 3.0 by Oscar & Crystal Jones

Naked Sex (For Married Couples Only) by Oscar & Crystal Jones

No Longer A Dream: Step by Step Guide to Writing Your First Book by Crystal Jones

Not Without My Daughters: The Beginner's Guide to Mentoring and Being Mentored by Crystal Jones

Restore The Roar by Oscar Jones

Ring Talks by Oscar & Crystal Jones

The Newlywed Handbook by Oscar & Crystal Jones

The S Word: What Submission Is Not by Crystal Jones

Unafraid by Crystal Jones

When The Vow Breaks by Oscar & Crystal Jones

About Oscar & Crystal Jones

Oscar & Crystal Jones have been celebrating their covenant love affair for over 34 years. They have 7 children (which include 1 daughter- in-law and 1 son-in-law). They are also the happy grandparents of 8. Oscar & Crystal are both teachers by trade. They have both taught in the private and public sectors. Both have left the education system for full-time ministry. Apostle Oscar & Prophetess Crystal have a unique Aquila and Priscilla team ministry. They lavishly love the Lord and one another. God has coupled this into a special anointing and gifted them to be able to minister from the pulpit as one voice. They are founders of Marriage for a Lifetime Ministries. They are overseers of Greater Works Family Ministries, The Love Culture Christian Center and Agape International Association of Churches and Para-churches. The two have been featured guests on several radio and television broadcasts. The couple has authored several books together and apart. They aspire to leave a legacy of hope and healing to the body of Christ.

The couple presently reside in Atlanta, GA.

Contact info:

Agape International Association of Churches and Parachurches

website: www.theclergy.org
email: agape@theclergy.org

Oscar & Crystal Jones
19136 Joy Road
Detroit, MI 48227

www.ingramcontent.com/pod-product-compliance
Lightning Source LLC
LaVergne TN
LVHW051153080426
835508LV00021B/2602